The Leading Trees

& other story poems

Melinda B Hipple

The Leading Trees

First Publication Credits

"The Leading Trees" - Pirene's Fountain, Jan. 2008
Commended in the 2008 Margaret Reid Poetry Prize
for Traditional Verse
"The Sparrow Found Him First" - Pirene's Fountain, Oct. 2008
"Fox and Goose" - Citation in the 2008 NFSPS Games Competition
"Chrysalis" - Pirene's Fountain, Oct. 2009
"Abstractions" - Pirene's Fountain, May 2009,
nominated for Editor's Prize
"Religioso" - Pirene's Fountain, Oct. 2010,
nominated for Editor's Prize
"Enchantment" - Winner of the 2012 Sonnet Poetry Competition

Copyright © 2018 by Melinda B Hipple
ISBN 978-1-64254-334-6

Second Edition © 2020 by Melinda B Hipple
All rights reserved. No part of this publication may be reproduced, distributed, or transmitted in any form or by any means, including photocopying, recording, or other electronic or mechanical methods, without the prior written permission of the copyright holder, except in the case of brief quotations embodied in critical reviews and certain other noncommercial uses permitted by copyright law. For permission requests, write to the publisher, addressed "Attention: Permissions Coordinator," at the address below.
ISBN: 978-1-64318-105-9

Cover image: *Blossoming Almond Tree* by Vincent van Gogh
In the Public Domain

703 8th Street
Baldwin City, KS, 66006
www.imperiumpublishing.com

Poems

- 5   The Leading Trees
- 10   Lady of Plain
- 15   The Sparrow Found Him First
- 19   Rebecca Moore
- 24   The Art Lesson
- 28   A Fairy Dream
- 39   Chrysalis
- 42   In Glory's Name
- 46   King of the Macabre
- 51   Fox and Goose
- 54   The Last Ray of Sun
- 56   Abstractions
- 57   Religioso
- 58   The Bounty Here
- 59   Enchantment

The Leading Trees

for Barbara

As stoic sentinels, they wait for me
o'er lane beneath the shadow of their arch.
These trees that once were proudly kept do see
how time, relentless, never slows its march.

They call with silent beckoning—their twigs,
the distant, outstretched limbs of mother's arms.
But close, their dark embrace is but a prig
to steal my peace, so toxic are their charms.

These blackened trees, with blacker hearts
                                        to match,
adorn the ruthless white of sun-drenched snow
and pull, with ties my childhood did attach,
entreating me to face an ancient foe.

A hollow place of blood relations, home.
So, why is there this need to reconcile
a past so fetid that I have to comb
through years of buried truths extremely vile?

At twelve, I was unspoiled and newly bloomed.
The green of spring just budding from each limb
cast shadows long to cool the lane consumed
by laughter, shoeless feet and childish whim.

But summer honey turned to bitter tang
when autumn stole my father from my life.
The midnight hearse crept by as heartache sang.
The trees bent low as though consumed by strife.

November wind rang hollow through the trees,
reminding Mother of her lover lost.
Her empty arms clutched wildly at the breeze
to grasp another, but her heart was frost.

She drew a man, I will not say his name
(the fifteen elms did shudder when he passed).
He had no wish to thaw her heart with flame.
Instead, he sought to hold her sorrow fast.

He used her pain to gain a stranglehold,
as puppeteer, controlling what she'd see,
and with the blinders quite secure, stone-cold,
he turned attention and his lust to me.

Through winter nights as chill as polar ice,
I fought to keep my heart above the dread.
I prayed the leading trees would soon entice
a savior knocking, knowing the unsaid.

Without a word, he'd pluck me from the door
and cast a golden lance into the thief
who dared defile a child, then he'd restore
my mother's heart, releasing it from grief.

I prayed the leading trees would soon entice.
I prayed upon my father's bleeding soul.
I prayed until my own heart turned to ice.
I prayed until the silence took its toll.

At seventeen, I passed between the elms
one final time, their branches sick with blight.
My father's ghostly hand reached from a realm
where restless souls are driven still to fight.

He punished root and bark and sagging bough
for failing justice, failing to defend
his daughter. As I passed, I heard him vow
my vengeance in the whisper of the wind.

The lengthy shadow of the elms did reach
from continent to continent. Desire
for peace was never stronger than the leech
of hate that was this all-consuming fire.

True peace was a mirage upon the sand,
and though I left the man without a soul,
I never lost the image of the hand that
could have stopped the damage, kept me whole.

And now she calls to me with dying breath—
a mother lost, a woman with regret.
But who am I to sanctify her death
while Father's breezes whisper, "Don't forget."

And yet, I'm here. I stand before these trees
to watch them shudder in the bitter frost,
their hearts still black. I still recall my pleas
unanswered from a childhood long since lost.

Forgiveness. Is that something I can give
the dying? Do I want to know her heart,
or do I find it safer that I live
still damaged by the weakness on her part?

I hate the man who crept into my bed
pretending that his love was something pure,
and yet he'd never had my trust. The dead
will reckon with his tortured soul, I'm sure.

But what of Mother—loved and loving wife,
betrayer of the child when asked to choose?
Her failing cut much deeper than the knife
I use to slice away his damned abuse.

An odium so strong it smells of musk
draws deep from me desire to turn and run.
The leading trees turn gray with coming dusk,
and I must choose to save us both, or none.

Lady of Plain

A pauper, you may think. A soul denied.
My face so etched by want and sacrifice
has seen its share of heartache, paid a price
surrendering my birthright to my pride.

From noble blood, my coddled youth was meant
to shape a flawless, lordly bride. My fate—
to be the token played in games of state,
my wishes never questioned in consent.

At twelve, my house was chosen. Even so,
my groom was but a distant fantasy
embroidered with a silk naivety
and gilded in such dreams as girls do know.

The years till my betrothal flew like dust
in need of rain. I longed for fairytales
to sweep my virgin heart into the veils
of new romance—such adolescent lust.

Painting by Balthasar Denner

The unkind truth would shatter innocence.
The day of my engagement was at hand.
A gentleman of breeding would command
my father offer up his tithe at once.

A daughter's purity was paid, exchanged
in barter for security of class.
"It is our lot." My mother smiled. "Alas,
my marriage to your father was arranged."

I knew what was expected, but I'd read
of love so true, of kindred hearts so sure
that meeting sparked a passion strong and pure.
At seventeen, I craved the marriage bed.

By eighteen, I was loathed to see his face.
A comely man my groom turned out to be,
but with an ogre's heart. I wrote my plea
in letters home. *Please, save me this disgrace!*

I penned my anxious words by candlelight
and secreted the posts through messengers
that Husband would not know. The harbingers
of doom began a mantra of my plight.

My life became less bearable, my hope
soon dashed the day I found my letters stashed
in Husband's escritoire—my freedom cached
in bundles neatly tied with satin rope.

Not one had made it to my father's eyes.
The blame that I had harbored for his lack
of heed began to grow as fear. The black
of chamber walls did suffocate my cries.

My gilded cage was not the prize I thought.
Remembering my mother's face, I knew
at once her hollow gaze was sentence true
for privilege of class—such damage wrought.

My mother erred in nurturing a will
that would not cower to the rule of lords.
The more I pressed, the harsher my rewards.
If I remained, my spirit he would kill.

My silks, my satin pinafores and gold
all left behind, I walked with only wool
to guard my back. My husband lost a fool
as wife, but gained as widower condoled.

The rumor was, at water's edge, I slipped
and lost my foot into the briny deep—
a lie that was my benefit to keep.
My name so died upon the manor's crypt.

A pauper, that I am, but one with pride.
I hold my secrets close to hide my sin
from everyone but he who took me in—
a farmer needing field hands and a bride.

"My Lady, Plain," he calls me in the night
and rubs my calloused hands as we reflect.
No passion here, but comfort in respect
does bind the love we've fashioned in our right.

A bitter lord grows old alone, reviled
for baseless cruelty and wanton greed.
This woman worn, this wretch reborn in need
did raise his only son a pauper's child.

The Sparrow Found Him First

for Paul

A sparrow sang of grief today. In blue, the sky
bowed reverently as August held its breath.
The willow wept her draping tears. She knew
a mother's dread would soon by overwhelmed
                                    by death.

A roiling summer storm had left its mark
upon the town of Cooper's Bay. The sirens wailed
to send the timid fleeing. Dogs would bark
at mayhem in the air as twisted winds prevailed.

A funnel tore the town apart, then died. In silence,
huddled eyes stared out from houses caved upon
themselves. The weakest stayed inside. The brave
would venture first to see what God had saved.

They fell into the streets, too numb to think.
Young children ran to find their friends and share
the thrill of living through catastrophe—too soon to
blink. By grace, it seemed, no injuries were
                                    suffered, still.

A boy of twelve found courage quick. He raced
into the sunny peace, the afternoon turned clear.
Adventure could be had if he made haste. For
bragging rights, he combed the swollen river near.

His mother called his name until she bled. The
splintered town so torn by gale raised new alarms
as sirens wailed again with nervous dread,
this time for rescuers. The homeless came
                                        in swarms.

They scoured every inch of rubbled town. They
searched the hills and valleys wrecked by cyclone
hands again, with lanterns, when the sun went
down. By morning, weary souls were bowed by
                                        fear's demands.

The sparrow found him first. His mother cried.
Old willow brushed a tender leaf across his skin,
and when his mother stumbled to his side, young
sparrow cocked an eye and flew into the glen.

As mother held her blue-gray son and wept,
a gentle rhythm rose among the grass and trees.

She wailed despair, refusing to accept
the comfort offered by the willow and the breeze.

The town of Cooper's Bay had lost a son.
Surviving hail and brutish wind, the townsmen
sighed until their luck was changed. Their triumph
won had spun into a silence they could not abide.

The sparrow sings of grief today. In blue, the sky
bows reverently as summer holds its breath.
The willow weeps her draping tears anew
each time a mother's dread is overwhelmed
          by death.

Rebecca Moore

A stunning black on black, this night blows cold.
The bitter winds attack resolve, so brash
to penetrate the confidence I hold
at arm's length. I've never felt so old.

I stumble, quake on hallowed ground for more
than reason can explain. I do implore,
if I should fail to save myself, at least
know this—I shall have saved Rebecca Moore.

This day, this chilling night that bears no light,
has drawn me to a place of fools. I fight
the urge to pull away. I pray for strength
but, lo, in darkness even I'm contrite.

Rebecca, poor Rebecca, maiden pure.
Her heart was new to love, her pledge unsure.
I reasoned it would matter not that I
had motives darker than this waif demure.

Emilian School Portrait of a Lady

Her innocence was part the sport. In truth,
her purity the prize I sought, her youth
enticement for a soul as old as sin—
an appetizer for my thirsty tooth.

I pierced her skin the night she came to heed
her racing pulse, to consummate our tryst.
A virgin lost in suffocating need.
A virgin still, but bound to one of greed.

I drew her blood, her youth, her life to me.
I tapped the succor from her graceful neck
bent low. She suffered lust and agony
as I staked claim—her savior dark to be.

And now she's tied forever to the stars,
but with her ruin I have found my heart.
Three hundred years I've shadowed love apart
from life. I'll not condemn her to blackheart.

She stands before me, begging my embrace,
her features pale and fragile as the lace
that drapes her shoulder. "I have more to give,"
she pledges, tracing scars below her face.

I tense with yearning, wishing this abyss
would flood with burning life from just one kiss.
But drawn I am to darkness, and I fall
upon her flesh to drink in bloody bliss.

She sighs to me, "How can I live within
this longing. Take my soul to be as one,"
her breath a chilling wisp upon my skin.
From blackness, courage fires. I see my sin.

I draw from rectitude, and from my vest
I pull a stake of mighty oak. Her breast,
so tender 'neath the lace, breathes deep the shock.
Her fireless eyes now burn with flame possessed.

Rebecca struggles free, but I impose
a muscle garnered from a thousand deaths.
A distance greater than a man can close,
I leap! Her strength's exhausted in the throes.

With power of intent, I spin her 'round.
I plunge the stake full thrust. My god the sound
of crushing bone and screaming flesh! And now,
the silence. Dreadful silence does abound.

She falls, a fresh coquette across my arm,
her dead eyes fading, having lost their charm.
At last, they've won salvation from a life
that mimics death. I have undone the harm

so done to me. Though wickedness was mine
right from the start, not so, Rebecca. Fine
in form and fine in heart she'll always be.
But as for me, alas, . . . there's only time.

The Art Lesson

"Like this," he said, his steady hand so sure
to sketch the line of lip and graceful chin.
I reveled in the accolade as muse
to one so brilliant with an artist's pen.

"I love the way strong daylight shadows deep
your tuliped mouth." His fingers touched a spark,
a gentle blush upon my skin. "Now turn
to let me catch the sun before it's dark."

His charming smile would fail to reach his eyes
intent on drawing truth from rag and ink.
What truth, I wondered, had an apple dreamed?
What certainty lie buried in white zinc?

I posed that summer, taking on the task
of goddess, mistress and a sprite or two.
My face would decorate commissioned oils
a dozen-fold, his passion in the hue.

Obsession did begin as faint desire,
but how could I resist the compliment
of someone so intent upon my shape
to render it as Venus, love's lament?

One noon, as we shared sweetbreads over break,
he asked, "Would it be proper to impose
upon your modesty, my dear. I feel
your beauty has undone me with each pose."

"Why, yes," I said. "Whatever do you wish?"
my own heart yearning for his gentle stroke.
"A classic nude," he whispered to his tea.
He smiled and added, "Something quite baroque."

As autumn tipped the sun and nights grew long,
the candlelight became my only cloth.
I bathed in richness from his doting gaze.
My splendor drew his fervor like a moth.

The passion rose between us like a pyre,
igniting something in his tortured heart.
By night, we filled each other's burning need.
By day, he poured it all into his art.

In time too swift, the painting was complete.
I felt a private showing was at hand.
His masterwork—a gift to me, adorned
with kisses and, I prayed, a wedding band.

The day I climbed the stairs to my demise,
I found him with a patron, sharing wine.
They tipped a glass and laughed at how naive
the beauty was now gracing canvas fine.

A wind as hot as Hades charred my bones.
I grabbed the nearest weapon I could find
and fell upon the painting, tearing holes
to shred the last of dignity maligned.

But that was not enough to ease my ache.
The brush that so revealed my naked soul
was there, within my grasp. I snatched it up
and drove it deep into his eyes of coal.

I wait for sentence, now, a murderous tart
immortalized in stunning oils—my dearth
of luck exaggerated by his fame.
It seems, I nearly doubled what he's worth.

Painting by Paul Jacques Aimé Baudry

A Fairy Dream

As fine a fairy ring as Nim had seen grew circles
in the fresh-mown meadow grass. Each mushroom
gleamed snow white against the green
of dazzling dew. The morning sun shown brass.

On bended knee, he searched the dew-damp soil
for tiny tracks, small footprints left behind.
A perfect moon had been night's perfect foil
to light the rarest wonder of its kind.

He knew the ring and moon aligned in fate,
exposing secret passage to a realm
where creatures mystical would congregate—
a fairy festival between the elm.

If Nim had found the ring before new dawn, he
might have spied their carnival of dance, but
sunlight broke the spell. The sprites were gone.
To find another ring would be such chance.

When he was young, a boy of only four,
his mother's mother sang a wondrous song
as lullaby. The tale he did adore
soon stirred a dream of wanting to belong.

Though years of searching never found a clue,
young Nim determined myth was often based
on fragile truth that time could misconstrue.
In legend, possibility was laced.

A sound, a tiny mewing caught his ear,
and Nim turned quick from memory to find
a small enchantress sitting very near.
Around her fragile wings, a vine entwined.

"Be true!" he cried into the morning air.
"I dare not blink or she will disappear!"
He knelt much closer, being quite aware
that this could be hallucination queer.

"Unwind me, please," a little voice spoke up.
"Since you have found me, set me free, I plead."
Nim reached, and in his trembling hands did cup
a creature glowing amber. "True, indeed!"

His eyes took in a nymph no bigger than
a wood thrush dressed in voile of shimmered gold.
Her burnished copper tresses overran
her shoulders. Such a marvel to behold!

He pulled the vine from 'round her gauzy wings
and brought her close. "My dear, you are a sight,
a valued prize my patience surely brings."
"A prize!" she quipped. "How very impolite."

"My pardon, but I truly must implore
your services. A fairy wish, you see,
is what I would possess, and so before
I set you free, I claim what comes to me."

The pixie shook her head, and lustrous sparks
of dust fell from her auburn hair. She laughed
in trilling notes that caused the song of larks
to echo from the trees. "You must be daft!"

"No other has command of Man's desire.
A want is yours to wish and make come true."
But Nim held fast to childhood fancy's fire.
"I wish to live enchanted, just like you."

"Like me?" she asked, and insight crossed her
face. "To render magic as a way of life,
commune with nature's wondrous charm and
grace, make mischief, never know a day of strife?

"Would this be what my charms should now
bestow?" "Oh, yes," said Nim as hunger filled his
core. "My wish—that mystery was mine to know.
Let magic fill my life, I do implore!"

The little nymph consented with a grin.
"A bargain, then, for you must earn this right.
In ten years hence return to this same glen
when May's full moon shines brightest in the night.

"Please bring the thing most precious to your
heart, for I require a treasure in return.
It's only then I'll grant a life apart
from Man. Indeed a fairy's life you'll earn.

Disheartened, Nim released his prisoner
and watched her sail a distance from his hand.
She hovered like a bee, her wings a blur.
"Return," she said. "Your wish I will command."

With that, a doorway opened in the air.
The cherished imp then curtsied her retreat.
A wide-eyed Nim had witnessed something rare,
and yet, he found the meeting bittersweet.

A decade, still, to live a childhood dream
would seem eternity to one so young.
His patience thin, he struggled to redeem
his thought with memory of passage sung.

Li lo li lo, the merry moon shines fair
upon a ring of magical delight.
Li lay li lay, a fairy ring is there.
It calls to imp and nymph and woodland sprite.

He left the meadow, gone to live his life,
forgetting not the promise to be kept.
When, later, love brought Nim a caring wife,
he sang to her by moonlight as she slept.

Li lo li lo, they sing of life so sweet,
beguiling tunes that cast entrancing spells.
Li lay li lay, the time to spy is fleet,
as morning peals her birdsong in the dells.

A daughter fair was born to bring him joy
the likes of which he'd never known before.
A radiance not seen since ancient Troy,
her lullabies were filled with ancient lore.

Li lo li lo, a fairy's life for me
should providence provide the willing arms.
Li lay li lay, from strife I would be free
should I be granted Puck's enchanting charms.

A decade passed before the time was felt.
A wiser Nim returned to meadow's place
where memory recalled a fairy dwelt.
He held his sleeping child in tight embrace.

The moon shone gleaming on the grassy field,
but nowhere did it light a fairy ring.
He sighed relief—his vague regret concealed—
and to the darkness, Nim began to sing.

Li lo li lo, my willing heart sings true
a tale of magic spun upon the wind.
Li lay li lay, the trace of morning dew
will bring this fancy's seeking to an end.

And as the father turned away his dream,
a spark of light flew close from meadow's edge.
A golden fairy, auburn hair agleam,
spoke soft. "Dear Nim, is this the gift you pledge?"

"The gift," said Nim, "is only that you see
the beauty blessed to one so human, still,
and know that I release your pledge to me.
No longer do I ask for your good will.

"For I have found the magic that I sought
communing with my daughter's impish soul, and
though not free of strife, her life has taught that
wondrous charm and grace has made me whole."

The pixie's aura deepened ruby red,
and Nim pulled back, afraid that he had come.
"I'll not release this precious gift," he said,
"no matter to what fate I shall succumb!"

A birdsong laughter pealed into the night
as fairy dust shook loose from tresses charmed.
"This pact," she cried, "was never ours to write.
I only wished to slip away unharmed!

"Suggestion to a stubborn youth whose eyes
had not yet seen enough of life to show
that living human is the greatest prize.
For love is something fairies cannot know."

Unearthly quiet fell upon the pair,
and in his arms, the child began to stir.
Her bright eyes widened at the glow midair.
"Oh, Papa! Is the fairy song of her?"

"It is," said Nim, his eyes alive with glee.
"She's come to wish us well in all we do.
I hope she will forgive a fool," said he.
"Forgiven." Pixie smiled. "For friendships new."

Until new morning's glow, the fairy danced,
cascading pixie dust in rainbow shades.
A father and his daughter stood entranced.
At last the fairy said, "This night now fades,

"and soon I must retreat to mystic lands
where magic reigns, but don't forget this night
and what you learned. The human heart commands
supreme enchantment. Love is your delight."

With that, she cast her fairy dust upon
the beaming child. "A life of charm you'll know."
She turned and flew into the coming dawn
as heartfelt tears began to flow.

Li lo li lo, Nim whispered soft and sweet.
His daughter's head began to nod with sleep.
A fairy's life is sadly incomplete.
Li lay li lay, my human form I'll keep.

Li lo li lo, the years have taught me well—
to savor joy, one must have tasted strife.
Li lay li lay, a fairy wise can tell,
to render magic is to love this life.

Chrysalis

for Roxine

Wisps of cirrus stroked the heavens, chastening
September's cobalt skies—those hues which sting
the eyes on brighter afternoons. The news was
doom. We stood, my friend and I, in weight of
silence

while each passerby would nod a greeting, smiling,
then would motivate their step to leave us be.
Perhaps we should have mourned more privately.
No tears, and yet, the pall was thick as winter fog.

That morning's call had left me stunned, a hollow
growing around my heart from fear, but vexing
more at how a cosmic plan would dare be this
unjust, so sure this woman suffering endured
enough.

What past-life sins could strap her to a body
broken so, to suffer through and gain her strength
of soul, her true conviction in what must be good,
then wave reward just moments shy of gifting
ruin?

For forty years, their love—postponed but now deserved—had been preserved until two hearts were strong enough to know the good of what their joining meant, two weak hearts tempered through the living fires.

No sooner had desire been given chance to flame than she would know her death—her lungs to lose their breath in increments while he'd be made to bear this cross as widower again.

My friend and I, we spoke of this as though his cross was harder. In a daze, my gaze picked up a passing fleck, a darkened movement in the air just as the reaper flew it there.

"Oh, look!" my friend cried out. "A sign, perhaps to lift your spirits." And the darkness bloomed into a butterfly. I shrugged the thought, but kept my eyes transfixed upon its wings.

Deep fascination drew me. Was it death or was it life—this darkened symbol that now flew directly to me. Blackness flitted near our heads. The more it stayed, the more I stared. What beauty could this harbinger expect me to accept? No matter what I did believe, my heart still wept. The butterfly brought focus to the silence on the sidewalk at my feet and rested there.

This omen still seemed happenstance, and so I thought a test of just how random was its lighting near. I stooped to press my hand upon the ground while no one made a sound.

These wings of death, embellished by the cobalt skies, did not tremble at my offering, the nimble, thin thread legs made sure-foot steps toward my fingers, never hesitating once to take their place.

I raised the wisp toward my face and stood in easy wonder. Afraid to shake it loose, but still, I turned my hand to push all doubt aside. It clung . . . until I knew what truth it pledged.

A tender heart, a woman cruelly tied to pain, would be released upon the firmament to manifest a resonance in time—from damaged chrysalis to butterfly sublime.

In Glory's Name

I'll tell you, 'fore you go, young man,
it ain't quite what it seems. The dreams
of honor fall away, lose hand
when that first metal jacket screams.

You thought you knew though, didn't you?
I saw it in your eyes—that fire,
that hankerin' for glory due.
Here's news, boy. Hormones do conspire

to dumb you down about the time
they fill you up with impudence.
You're ripe for pickin' by the slime
that has more clout than common sense.

The things they ask of you and me
in different wars are still the same—
to take their word as guarantee
that who you're killin' needs no name.

A boy of nineteen years I was,
a pissant youngster out for blood.
Adrenaline was flowing 'cause
the tension was as thick as mud.

The blackest night had left us blind,
our heartbeats poundin' like a drum.
We found a berm to lay behind
and tried to slow our breathin' some.

The sounds of jungle pricked our ears,
our hearing now acutely fixed
on anything that fed our fears.
The silence held us all transfixed.

Was just a snap. A single twig
no bigger than my fingertip.
When hell broke loose, I took a swig
of courage as I firmed my grip.

The AKs fired a tracer wall
to open wide the devil's door.
I felt the bullet's stealthy crawl
through bone and muscle just before

my heart exploded in my chest.
I blinked, and there we stood in light—
two soldiers' bodies dispossessed.
His Asian face seemed all too slight.

We watched a medic give me aid
until his arms were achin' sore.
My buddies stumbled out and sprayed
more rounds into the Asian's core.

But he and I were past a care,
now wonderin' what we fought about.
My side and his still both declare
the right of what their doctrines spout.

It ain't no different in the sand
where teenage children play the game
of warrior led by the hands
of selfish men, their spots the same.

I've been to Egypt, Senegal,
Columbia and Kosovo,
Nagorno. Yes, I've seen 'em all,
the young caught in the undertow.

There's nothing here to fill my day
'cept greetin' new boys past the veil.
I've tried to send the word your way,
but hate keeps messin' with the mail.

You hear me now, I know you do—
your eyes upon the other side.
You're holdin' dogma past its due.
A shame it is that both sides lied.

So, as you lay there bleedin' through,
expecting you're to be redeemed,
remember, war is hell, it's true.
And glory sure ain't what it seemed.

King of the Macabre

As chilly winds whipped by the man in black,
he grasped his hat and leaned into the gale.
With not enough to guard his shivered back,
he ducked into a tavern serving ale,
adjusting to the air both warm and stale.

So dim the light, he took a moment's time
to gather his surroundings. At the bar,
a scattering of patrons dropped a dime
for one more round. A woman tipped the jar
as she removed herself and her cigar.

"And what for you?" the barkeep asked as he
wiped dry an empty glass. "How 'bout a beer?"
The man took off his coat and said, "Chablis."
He found an empty stool to park his rear
and took in all the charming atmosphere.

"You gotta name? The keep asked as he poured.
"I'm Edgar," said the man who tipped his glass,
relieving it of wine. He then implored
another drink. "I find this vintage crass.
Is there a better label with more class?"

"Be careful," said a man on Edgar's right.
"The barkeep doesn't take to insults well.
You might be asking for a barroom fight."
He reached a friendly hand to break the spell.
"I'm Stephen. Welcome to our little hell."

The barkeep pulled a bottle from the shelf.
"It's fifty bucks, if this be what you want."
"It would, and I will have it to myself,"
said Edgar waiving money, nonchalant.
He eyed the vintner's name—Château le Monte.

"The bottom half tastes better than the top,"
said Stephen, smiling at this rube. "Hip hip."
He raised his bottled beer to toast the fop.
First Edgar eyed the man, then took a sip.
"You called this Hell. Please, do explain that quip."

"Ah," Stephen sighed. "You wish to know this lot.
Well, there is much to tell. You see this gent?"
and Stephen slapped the shoulder of a sot
who sat beside him. "His predicament—
he sees the future since his accident."

"Tis nothing," scoffed old Edgar with a grin.
"For I have known a man who hears a heart
through floorboards after his most heinous sin."
"A trifle," Stephen laughed. "A world apart
from Barkeep's wife—a car that can outsmart."

"A fantasy," said Edgar. "Rings untrue.
A premise quite ridiculous, unlike
orangutans that terrorize a Rue."
He poured another glass, his mind to psych.
The barkeep laughed. They were so much alike.

"It's apes you want? Then here's one. Let's talk
pets," and Stephen's eyes began to dance a bit.
"Oh, nonsense," Edgar stated. "One forgets,
our greatest fear is Man on Man. Admit,
you'd cower at the pendulum and pit!"

"Then this!" cried Stephen standing from his stool,
"has got to be the ultimate. A girl
whose mind can act upon her hate at school."
But Edgar yawned and gave his wine a twirl.
"Contrivance. Inner fear is horror's pearl,

as simple as a bird in black, you see."
He tipped the final drop of wine and smiled.
"A raven, yes who taps incessantly
reminding us of private demons riled.
True terror needs no foolish trappings wild."

A silence fell as Stephen bowed defeat
while Edgar donned his coat and felt chapeau.
"A pleasure, Mr. King, that we should meet.
You're good." Ed winked. "As horror writers go."
He tipped his hat, then out walked Mr. Poe.

Fox and Goose

for Jim

In quiet grace, a snow fell overnight—
a wonderland revealed at morning light.
With noses pressed against the chilly pane,
we marveled at how flawless the terrain.

A steaming breakfast, followed by a race
to bundle up. In layers, just my face
would catch the bitter air as we escaped
outside. Once there, we simply stood and gaped.

"Who's first?" my brother asked, and I replied,
"The both of us. We each can take a side."
We leapt together, hand in hand, to land
a distance out. In smoothest snow we'd stand.

Then back to back, we started scooching feet.
Our semi-circled paths came round to meet.
We dug the trail as big as room allowed,
and then we'd plot the crosstrails to be plowed.

"This snow is deeper than the one last year,"
I huffed as clouds of vapor did appear.
"I think this is the best we've ever made,"
said Jim. His eyes would twinkle as we played.

Our yard, indeed, was biggest on the street.
For Fox and Goose, it was the place to meet.
Soon children from around the block would come
to challenge us until their toes grew numb.

Midmorning, there were dozens in the match,
all vying for the role as fox to catch
the goose (or geese, as case may be). We'd flee
the fox through snowy maze and laugh with glee.

The biting cold began to take its toll
as some were tagged and others reached the goal.
But one by one, the players would give in
to brother-sister tactics, and we'd win.

Defeated, cold and hungry, most would leave,
while one or two more hearty did believe
that they could take us on in other games.
But soon, their victories went up in flames.

Each mother called her child in from the cold—
those warriors defeated by the bold.
Now Jim and I, triumphant, would retreat
into the warmth of home and our conceit.

Reliving tales of glory, we replayed
each battle won as day began to fade.
Our supper soon inhaled, we found our beds
and let the satisfaction fill our heads.

Outside, the streetlight threw a pallid glow
upon the trails in desecrated snow.
But as we slept, a silent flurry fell
to set the stage and cast another spell.

The Last Ray of Sun

in memoriam

The young man stands aghast before his mother
and offers up his soul with each new tear.
Before he found the gun, he'd had a brother
where now a single echo rings austere.

Though not the first this mother knows of grieving,
she knows the burden falls upon her son.
She should alleviate the sorrow heaving
in tender years, the stone of guilt begun.

How hard she fights the resonance of death
in remembering her first, a stillborn child.
Her second loss, a daughter just a year
when a birthday candle touched the babe beguiled.

And now her second son is lost to shrapnel,
debris from grownup toys in children's hands.
It matters not that death was accidental.
The stain of killing bleeds its own demands.

A mother/son relationship is bonding
in grief so poison even loving stings.
The third son's light is fading—now responding
to suffering times three and how it clings.

Abstrations

He presses crumbling graphite deep, the white
of heavy texture grips each forceful line.
Suggestions of a brawny form excite
his frantic hand to grandly redefine
the flesh and blood of life upon the page.
Reality dissolves just past the muse.
Would this, a caustic piece, perhaps engage,
enrage the academe's elitist views?
No matter. His is not to fashion tripe.
Instead, he guts his soul and spills it raw
onto the wall of shadows, smears a swipe
of sore emotion drawn from passion's craw.

He dares the critic's eye to search beyond
abhorrence, grasp where truth and beauty bond.

Religioso

Ink dewdrops on a spinner's web, these notes
upon a staff ring clear, precarious
as silken thread. A winding vine denotes
which clef the maestro's Stradivarius
will choose to orchestrate the summer's heat.
Divining wind plays reeds around a marsh
while oboe charms in melodies petite.
A mimic of the grandiose or harsh
or sanguine or sublime, we stand transfixed,
transformed by timbre in the heart. Profound
the sound of Berlioz and birds when mixed:
omaggio and God's own voice are bound.

When music mimes what heaven does extol,
a note to shatter glass can mend a soul.

The Bounty Here

Dead flat this land no matter where I faced,
a place of sand and nettles dried to bone with
scarce a branch to shade the sun-drenched stone.
This barren scape my heart had not embraced.

A stranger here, my life had been misplaced—
some cosmic slip for which I would atone.
I longed for verdant hills, not sky alone,
but my misgivings soon would be erased.

On nights so clear I hear the Milky Way,
I raise my eyes to watch the prize unfold
and see the inky heavens drop their tears.
In unobstructed views of cosmic play
the Leonids give chase, and I behold
great wonders falling down around my ears.

Enchantment

To dream of you is yet a life fulfilled,
a bud upon the willow not yet bloomed.
Forever caught in Spring's enchantment, stilled,
I wait to tender love lest I'm consumed.

This reverie in stasis will not yield
to Summer's coaxing, nor succumb to lust
as heat of passion born too soon does wield
a fiery death, thus charring dreams to dust.

But want if true perfection holds at bay
the chance to grow content with one who's flawed?
While catkins' silken threads and I turn gray,
the truth of Autumn proves my dream a fraud.

    Young silver willow, come grow old with me
    in Winter's sleep where dreams will set us free.